THE OTHER SIDE

THE OTHER SIDE

STORIES OF CENTRAL AMERICAN
TEEN REFUGEES WHO DREAM OF
CROSSING THE BORDER

Juan Pablo Villalobos
Translated by Rosalind Harvey

FARRAR STRAUS GIROUX

NEW YORK

Farrar Straus Giroux Books for Young Readers
An imprint of Macmillan Publishing Group, LLC
120 Broadway, New York, NY 10271

Printed in the United States of America
Designed by Aimee Fleck
First edition, 2019
10 9 8 7 6 5 4 3 2 1
fiercereads.com

Library of Congress Cataloging-in-Publication Data
Names: Villalobos, Juan Pablo, 1973- author. | Harvey, Rosalind,
    1982- translator.
Title: The other side : stories of Central American teen refugees who dream
    of crossing the border / Juan Pablo Villalobos ; translated by Rosalind
    Harvey.
Description: First edition. | New York : Farrar Straus Giroux, [2019] |
    Identifiers: LCCN 2018058988 (print) | LCCN 2019004762 (ebook) |
    ISBN 9780374305741 (ebook) | ISBN 9780374305734 (hardcover)
Subjects: LCSH: Teenage refugees—Central America—Juvenile literature. |
    Teenage immigrants—Central America—Juvenile literature. | Central
    America—Emigration and immigration—Juvenile literature. | United
    States—Emigration and immigration—Juvenile literature.
Classification: LCC HV640.5.C46 (ebook) | LCC HV640.5.C46 V55 2019 (print) |
    DDC 305.235092/69140973—dc23
LC record available at https://lccn.loc.gov/2018058988

Our books may be purchased for promotional, educational, or business use. Please con-
tact your local bookseller or the Macmillan Corporate and Premium Sales Department
at (800) 221-7945 ext. 5442 or by email at MacmillanSpecialMarkets@macmillan.com.

CONTENTS

AUTHOR'S NOTE

These are true stories, and I consider this book to be nonfiction, although it employs some of the narrative techniques of fiction in order to protect the protagonists' identities. All the stories are inspired by the testimonies of ten immigrant minors, collected in separate interviews conducted in June 2016 in Los Angeles and New York. The names of the young people have been changed so as to preserve their anonymity.

THE OTHER SIDE

ERE
YOUR
DS?!

NICOLE AND KEVIN

WHEN THE IMMIGRATION OFFICER CALLED ME UP, HE SAID:

"Do you have kids?"

"Yes," I told him, "I have two."

This was toward the end of February 2014, and back then Kevin was sixteen years old and Nicole was still little, only ten.

And he asked me:

"Where are they?"

"In Guatemala," I said, because that's where they were: I had left them with their grandmother when I came to the United States in 2007.

"Who do they live with?" he asked.

"My sister," I told him.

They had lived with my sister ever since my mom was killed. Yeah, the gang had killed my mom. They killed her in her own home. They had been charging her a "tax" like they do in Guatemala. My mom used to pay it to them until one day she'd had enough and told them she wasn't going to pay any more. But they got their dues in the end: My mom paid them with her life. They killed her in her house. And then they killed my brother-in-law, who my kids thought of as their dad.

"Have you spoken to your children in the last few days?" the officer asked me.

"No," I told him, "my sister told me she'd given them permission to go on a trip."

"A trip?"

"Yeah," I said, "with school."

He was silent for a while, and you could hear him shuffling papers. Then he said the names of my children and asked me if that was what they were called. I told him it was, and he was silent again for a moment.

"No," he said at last, "your kids aren't in Guatemala."

"Sorry?" I said.

"Your kids are here," he said. "We've got them here, on the San Ysidro border."

NOW
GOING
SL
FOR

I'M
TO
EEP
ABIT

KIMBERLY

YOU CAN'T REALLY TELL WHAT TIME IT IS WHEN YOU'RE IN the freezer. Not even if it's day or night. The freezer is the cell they put you in after Immigration catches you. They call it the freezer because it's a really cold room, and the only thing they give you to put over yourself is a kind of metal blanket. It's so cold I'm getting a cramp in my leg, although the cramp is probably from standing up the whole time. When they shut me in here, there was no more space to sit, or to lie down and sleep, because all the girls were sleeping on the floor and there wasn't any room left.

"Psst, hey: Don't fall over," one of the girls says.

"What?" I ask, because I didn't understand what she meant and because I didn't see which girl said it.

There are a lot of people in this cell, maybe sixty or eighty, all girls around my age, or even younger. There are some really little girls here, too. I was in another freezer before. There, we were all mixed in together, boys and girls, and there wasn't any space to sit down or lie down there, either, because it was so full.

"You closed your eyes and you're about to fall asleep standing up," the girl lying at my feet says.

I rub my eyes to stop myself feeling so drowsy and, as the

girl sits up, quickly stretch my legs to try and get rid of the cramp.

"Sit down," she tells me.

I obey before she has second thoughts. When I sit down my back hurts, but at least I can rest my legs. I sit in front of the girl, dark-skinned like me, her hair all tangled and dirty because we can't have showers here, or even a wash. She must be the same age as me, or fifteen at most, anyway.

"I woke up because I was hungry," she says. "Aren't you hungry?"

I tell her I'm not, that when I'm scared I lose my appetite. Now I realize that in all these days, since I left my grandparents' house, I've hardly eaten anything. There were a few days when I don't think I ate anything at all, when we were on the bus and we didn't even stop to eat. Then I got sick in the house where we were waiting to cross the border. I got an upset stomach from eating all that Mexican food.

"Do you think they'll bring the food soon?" the girl asks me.

I tell her I don't know, that they only brought me in here a few hours ago and they haven't brought any food since then.

"Did they only just catch you?" she says.

"No," I say. "They caught me two days ago, but they sent me somewhere else first."

"What did they give you to eat there?" she asks.

"A carton of milk and an apple," I say.

"That's it?"

"That's it," I tell her. "Once in the morning, once at lunch, and the same thing at dinner. That's all they gave us."

"Here they give you a sandwich," she says. "And some juice. How old are you?"

"Fourteen," I say.

"Me too," she says.

I can tell by the way she speaks that she's from El Salvador like me, although I guess she's from the capital.

"My name's Kimberly," I tell her.

"Where are you from?" she asks.

"Ahuachapán," I tell her. "What about you?"

"Why don't you lie down?" she says. "If you like, I'll stand up for a bit so you can have a rest. But you'll have to let me lie back down."

She stands up and motions at me to lie on the floor. So I do.

— — —

"Hey, you: It's my turn now."

I open my eyes and see the ceiling of the freezer. The girl is bending over me, shaking my shoulders. I sit up and she settles down at my side.

"What did you say you were called?" she asks. "Sorry, I'm so hungry I forget stuff."

13

"Kimberly," I say, "but people call me Kim. You can call me Kim if you like. Did I sleep for long?" I ask.

"I don't know," she says. "It's impossible to tell the time in here, but it felt like ages to me because my feet are hurting now."

We both fall silent and I try to stir myself so that I can stand. I yawn and my head spins, as if I can't get enough air. I'm so tired I can hardly tell when I'm awake and when I'm asleep. The first night, in the other freezer, I didn't sleep at all, then later on I did; I'd fall asleep in fits and starts.

"The other freezer where I was before was worse," I say, playing for time. If we start chatting then maybe I can stay sitting down a while longer. "The place started to look like a garbage dump because people would just drop their apple cores on the floor and it never got cleaned. And they would drop their milk cartons, too. And I was ill, I had the flu really bad. I was in there for two days, and then they started listing the people they were going to move to the other freezer. They called my name and they put us on a bus and brought us here."

"Do you think they're going to send us back?" she asks me.

"Where to?" I say.

"I mean, are they going to deport us?" she says.

"I don't know," I say. But I don't tell her that I spent the first night crying, that I really wanted to go back to El Salvador. I

14

was thinking about my grandparents. I didn't tell her that if they asked me to sign the deportation papers I'd say yes. Ever since I crossed the river, I couldn't stop crying and crying and feeling really sad. And I kept thinking: *What am I doing here?*

"I remember this old man who fell into the water when we crossed the river," I tell the girl instead. "We were in the boat and they were taking us across, saying we had to get out really carefully and run over to the other side. And the old man couldn't get out, even though he wasn't that old, and so they picked him up and threw him into the water. He was completely drenched, and they just left him there. Nobody helped him, because you can't stay on the bank for long. We all ran off, they didn't tell us where we had to go, so we ran over to this hill, with trees all over the place. There was no path and we had to push our way through. It was pitch black, and no one had a flashlight or anything because they'd told us we couldn't bring anything with us.

"There were about thirty of us: there were some pregnant women, some really young kids, and we couldn't find a way out. A little boy was crying. We had to turn back around and find another path. I saw an old woman carrying a bottle of water and I asked her if I could have some and she wouldn't give me any. She said that she had to keep it for herself. I haven't forgotten that, that she wouldn't give me any water. We saw some lights off in the distance and walked toward them. The truth is I had no idea what we were supposed to do, which way we were supposed to go, nothing. Then suddenly a car appeared. It was the police."

"Now I'm going to sleep for a bit," she says abruptly, and starts to stretch to make me get up.

I get to my feet and feel that my legs are numb, or rather, I don't feel my legs at all. It's as if they've been cut off.

"But if they bring the sandwiches, wake me up," says the girl.

- - -

"Hey, you: It's my turn," I say in a low voice so as not to startle her, but the girl doesn't wake up.

I think it's been about two hours since she lay down and I've got a cramp in my legs again. At that moment the door to the cell opens and a woman pushing a cart comes in: It's the sandwiches. The girls begin to stir. I bend down and say into my friend's ear, "Wake up, they're handing out the food."

We grab a sandwich and a carton of juice and sit down to have lunch. Or breakfast, or dinner. Who knows what time it is. The sandwich has a slice of ham in it. The juice is orange.

"Where are you trying to get to?" asks the girl.

"To my mom," I say.

"But where exactly?" she says.

"Hempstead," I tell her.

"Where's that?"

"Near New York."

"And who did you live with back in El Salvador?"

"I lived with my grandparents on my mom's side," I say, "in Ahuachapán, and I was with my grandparents on my dad's side for a bit, too—they live in San Salvador. But before I came over here I was with my grandparents on my mom's side. I lived with my older sister and my little brother."

"What about your dad?"

"My dad left when I was really small; I never spoke to him at all, I didn't spend any time with him. My mom separated from him when she was pregnant with me. I went to live in San Salvador for a while because he was there, too. But while I was living there he didn't come and visit me, didn't call to ask how I was. So I would call him or go and see him at his place, because if I didn't go then we never saw each other. And because I was always with my grandma on my mom's side when I was little, I felt kind of empty when I left her, so that's why I decided to go back and live with her.

"Sometimes I think about the fact that neither of my parents are going to raise me, and that makes me really sad. Because my mom went to the United States when I was four. She's the one who's always been there for me—she would send money to my grandparents to help out. She was always looking out for me. But I can barely remember her because when she was in El Salvador, I was still really little. Sometimes I would cry about that, like, why can't I be near her?"

I eat the rest of my sandwich thinking about my grandparents and about what my mom would be like. Sometimes I try to imagine her, but I don't know what she looks like. If I ran into her on the street I don't think I'd recognize her. "The hardest thing that ever happened to me was leaving my grandparents," I tell her. "What about you?"

"I want to get to my mom," she tells me.

"And where's she?" I ask.

"In Arizona," she replies, brushing crumbs from her lap. "If you want to sleep for a bit you might as well do it now while I'm feeling a bit stronger. I'll be hungry again soon."

— — —

I wake up when the girl shakes me by the shoulders and tells me to calm down and stop shouting.

"Shhh, shhh," she says, "you have to be quiet."

"What happened?" I ask.

"I think you were having a nightmare," she says. "You started shouting. Anyway, it's my turn, you've been asleep for a while now and I can't stand up anymore."

I sit up and make room so she can get comfortable. I remember the nightmare; it's still in my mind.

"What were you dreaming about?" says the girl.

"Something really awful that happened to me on the way here," I say. "In Reynosa, on the border. I was in a house where there were a lot of people headed this way. People waiting. Every day people would arrive, and others would leave, because the place wasn't big enough for so many people. We were all waiting to cross over, but to me they kept saying, *Tomorrow, tomorrow*, and yet they never came to get me. There were mattresses on the floor and that's where we slept. They brought us burritos to eat and I got sick, I got a stomach bug. I could hardly eat. There were some older women there who looked after me. They told me to stay close to them, that they wouldn't let me sleep anywhere else because there were a lot of men around. But there was one night when one of the women got up, I don't know where she went, and a man came over and lay down right next to me. And he started saying nasty things to me. And he started coming closer as if he was after something else, as if he wanted to take advantage of me. And then I woke up one of the women and told her what was happening, and she argued with the man, stopped him from bothering me. And he got all defensive and said he wasn't doing anything. But the next day, when at last it was my turn to leave, he came outside with me and gave me a piece of paper and told me to hang on to it. He had given me his phone number. I screwed up the paper and I threw it in the trash."

"You were really lucky," the girl says.

I nod at her, and then we both fall silent. I look at all the girls lying on the floor, wrapped in their thin foil blankets; this is when it's coldest, it must be really early in the morning.

"My aunt made me get an injection before I left," the girl says suddenly, as if she's been thinking about it for a long time. "In case something happened to me, so I wouldn't get pregnant."

I wait to see if she says anything else, but she says nothing, and I understand perfectly what she's talking about.

"The school I was at had a prison next door where they locked up all the gang members," I tell her. "Whenever I got out of school all these guys were there. Guys who wanted to hurt us. They wanted us to get involved in bad things with them. They're always saying stuff to girls. Whenever I'd get out of school they'd be there waiting. I would come out with my friends and they'd tell us to go various places with them. They asked me lots of times, but I always said no. There are a lot of out-of-the-way places where they did their things. None of us wanted to. And if we refused, they'd threaten to do something to us. That's why I decided not to go to school anymore, because I became too afraid."

— — —

"The police stopped us again in Mexico," I say to the girl. Two or three days have passed, and now we have more space in the freezer, because some of the girls have been taken away. At least now we can both lie down or sit, or stretch our legs, or do whatever we want. Sometimes we lie down and as we get sleepy we tell each other things. Really, I'm the only one who talks, because she hardly ever tells me anything. But I prefer talking to her, because if I stay quiet I start thinking about my grandparents. And about my mom, about whether they've told her I'm locked up here yet.

"They'd stopped us a few times already," I continue. "When we were on the bus. The bus would slow down suddenly, then stop. We'd look out the window and see the police: the trucks and the men in their uniforms. Sometimes we'd be asleep, and they wouldn't say anything to us. They didn't wake us up. Maybe they thought we were Mexican. Other times they'd make us get off and ask for our papers. I showed them a birth certificate and an ID card from El Salvador. They'd ask us questions about what we were doing and who we were traveling with. Then they'd start asking for money. One cop would order another one to make us get off and handcuff us. They made as if they were going to arrest us and take us away, to frighten us. They'd say that unless we gave them the amount they were asking for, they would send us back right then and there. They'd deport us from Mexico. We'd give them the money we had on us and then they'd let us through."

At that moment, we hear the door to the cell opening and the girl practically leaps to her feet.

"They're going to feed us again," she says.

But they fed us not that long ago, so it must be something else. A woman immigration agent comes into the freezer and tells us that some of the girls are going to be transferred to a home in Phoenix. She says she has a list and is going to read out the names. She starts to read and then a few names later she says, "Kimberly," and my surname.

She stops reading and tells us that the girls on the list are to go with her. My friend tells me her name wasn't on the list, that she has to stay, and I realize she never told me what she was called.

"You didn't tell me your name," I say.

"It doesn't matter," she says, and gives me a hug.

THE
SIDE
THE
SI

OTHER
MEANS
OTHER
DE

SANTIAGO AND DANIEL

THE KID WAS WALKING ALONG, SWEATING BIG TIME, MAKING out he was totally oblivious, as if he didn't realize he'd just crossed over from the other side. But of course he knew— everybody knows; there's not a single person in Ilopango who doesn't know where the dividing line is, and that's why my guard went up. I thought: *This kid's plotting something, he must be a lookout for the Salvatrucha.*

He was eating a bag of potato chips and he was pretty heavy; I guessed he was around fifteen or sixteen—far too old to be acting so dumb. He had a backpack on and looked very dapper, with his brand-new jeans and his shirt all freshly pressed—I thought I'd better take a look and see what he had in his backpack, why he was going around all dressed up like that. I crossed the street and caught up with him.

"Psst, hey, stop where you're going," I said.

He turned and glanced quickly at me, kept on walking, all hoity-toity, slower now, but without stopping. If it was down to me I'd have stabbed him in the gut by now, burst that snooty bubble of his—no one can walk around pretending they can't hear someone from the 18th talking to them. Only thing is, I always get asked, "Who gave you authorization, who do you think you are, going above the guys at the top, you've got to take a good look at who it is before you take out your piece . . ."

"You'd better stop, kiddo," I said again, and grabbed him by the arm.

He stopped walking without looking at me and I could hear him breathing heavily: The kid was nervous. He knew who he was talking to and already his legs were starting to tremble.

"Are you ignoring me or what?" I asked him.

He said nothing, just carried on huffing and puffing like a horse. I shoved his shoulder and he fell against the wall, without putting up a fight. Sweat poured off his forehead like a fountain.

"Where are you going all dressed up?" I said.

He wiped the sweat away with a folded handkerchief he took from his pocket, and glanced around before replying, as if he were looking for someone. Unlucky for him: There were hardly any people out in the street, and the few who were walked past quickly so as not to get mixed up in any trouble. Everyone knows you don't get involved with M-18 just to stand up for some random kid.

"I know Yoni," the boy said, when he realized there was nothing to do but talk.

"Well, what a coincidence—so do I," I told him.

He tried to walk away, but I grabbed his arm and pushed him again.

"Seems to me you're a lookout for the Salvatrucha," I said.

He fell silent again, not saying a word, not even looking at me, just staring over at the end of the street as if he were going to find someone who would save him. The only thing this kid knew how to do was huff and puff like a horse.

"You think I didn't see you come from the other side?" I said. "The other side belongs to the Salvatrucha—don't make out you didn't know that. Everybody knows that. Where are you going?"

He took his handkerchief from his pocket and wiped his forehead again.

"What's the matter, you melting or something?" I said.

"Yoni's my friend," the fat kid said again. "Just ask him."

"I will ask him, but first you've got to tell me where you're going."

"I'm going home," he told me.

"Where do you live?" I asked.

"Around the corner," he said. "At the inn."

"And what were you up to on the other side, eh?" I said. "I think you're a lookout for the Salvatrucha."

"I went to do a school project," the kid said, pretending he wasn't a lookout at all. "A group project—one of the other kids in my group lives over there. I can show you what's in my bag if you like, so you can see."

He took off his backpack, undid the zipper, and showed me he was carrying books, paper, school stuff. He had another packet of potato chips in there, too.

"And your buddy's not in the Salvatrucha?" I asked him.

"I just went over to do my homework," he said. "Honest, ask Yoni, he knows me, he knows my family."

"OK, I will," I told him.

The boy was about to do up his backpack again, but I stopped him.

"Give me the potato chips," I said.

I grabbed the chips and gave Yoni a call. When he picked up you could hear the sound of the TV in the background really loudly; he must have been watching a film with his girl.

"Yoni, we've got a problem here," I said. "Can you hear me?"

Yoni must have paused the film because the racket stopped and all I could hear was his voice as he replied.

"Quickly then, I'm busy," he said. "What's up?"

"There's this kid on his way back from the Salvatrucha side and he says he knows you," I said.

"What's his name?" asked Yoni.

I asked the kid, who was wiping his forehead and his neck again, what his name was.

"Santiago," he said. "Tell him my grandma owns the shop, over there in the inn."

I repeated what he'd said to Yoni.

"Bring him here," Yoni said, and ended the call.

"Yoni wants to say hello," I told the boy.

I took him by the arm and started walking. The kid dug his heels in, and since he was so large it was hard to force him.

"My grandma's waiting for me," he said. "I have to help her in the shop."

"You can tell that to Yoni," I said. "Now get a move on, or you'll see what happens to you. It's not as if I don't know where you live."

I took out my knife and showed it to him. The kid averted his eyes, but he did start walking right away. We crossed several streets until we got to Yoni's place, with me eating the bag of potato chips on the way. I was starving because I'd been on lookout duty since early—since twelve o'clock—and it was nearly five now.

Yoni was sitting with his girl watching the movie, and they were eating pupusas. I'd seen the film before: It was the story of a little boy who could talk to dead people. Yoni pressed pause when he saw us come in and the boy immediately started accusing me.

"This guy's threatening me," he said to Yoni. "I was just coming back from doing my school assignment. It's not my fault my teacher put me in the same group as a kid who lives on the other side."

"He said he was your buddy, Yoni," I said, "but he was coming straight from where the Salvatrucha lot are—I saw him coming that way."

"His grandfather used to own the inn," Yoni told his girl. "The one around the corner—there was a time when my dad used to rent a room from him, but you don't rent rooms out anymore, do you?" he asked the kid.

"Not anymore," the kid replied. "When my grandfather died, my grandma decided that the inn would just be for the family."

"And who else lives there?" Yoni asked him.

"My great-grandma, my aunt, my uncles, and my cousins," he replied.

"Didn't you have a brother?"

"Yes."

"And how old is he?" Yoni asked. "He was called Daniel, wasn't he?"

"He's ten," the boy replied.

"And you?"

"Fifteen."

"Is your mom still in the U.S.?"

The kid said that she was and took his handkerchief out again to dry the sweat on his neck, his face, and his forehead. Yoni looked at him, a half smile on his lips, and squeezed his girlfriend's hand to get her to look at him, too.

"Everyone here in the neighborhood loves your grand-mother," he said. "We respect her, but you shouldn't take advantage of that if you don't want everyone to think you're a wimp."

Yoni's girlfriend burst out laughing, and so did I. The kid screwed up his handkerchief and stuffed it back in his pocket.

"I'm sick, Yoni," the boy said. "I've got something wrong with my heart—I had to go to the cardiologist because I get tired really quickly and I start to sweat."

"Are you serious?" Yoni asked.

The kid said that he was.

"I've got a big heart," he said, "bigger than normal."

"Sit down," said Yoni, and he gestured at a chair. "Don't you go fainting on me now."

"I can't stay long," said the boy. "My grandma's waiting for me: I have to work in the shop this afternoon and I'm already late because the assignment was really difficult and then this guy," indicating me, "stopped me."

Yoni got up from the sofa where he was sitting, left the plate of pupusas on the table, walked over to where the fat kid was, and pushed him down onto the chair.

"Did the Salvatrucha stop you?" he asked.

"They stop everyone," the kid replied, practically in tears.

"And what did you tell them?"

"Nothing."

Yoni clicked his tongue, exasperated by this point.

"Are you going to start blubbering now?"

He huffed and puffed again, but internally, like he was gulping down his snot.

"What did you tell them?" Yoni asked him again.

"They wanted to know where I was going, and they came with me to my friend's house," the kid said. "When they saw that I really was just going to do an assignment they left."

"You aren't lying to me, are you?" Yoni asked.

"No."

"You remember Marco?" Yoni said. "We caught him acting as a lookout for the Salvatrucha, and you know what happened to him."

Just then Yoni's phone rang, and he went into another room, so we couldn't hear him. The boy saw his chance and wiped his forehead with his handkerchief again. Then Yoni came back.

"I'm going to need you to hide something for me at the inn," he said.

"I can't," the kid said.

"There are loads of rooms there," Yoni said. "You're bound to find a safe place to put it."

The kid said nothing, didn't even look at Yoni while he was

34

talking; he just stared at the floor as if someone were going to burst up out of the ground to rescue him.

"It's just for a little while," Yoni said. "Until tomorrow."

"I can't, really I can't, Yoni," said the boy. "If my grandma finds out—"

"I'm not asking you," interrupted Yoni. "I've just been told the police are sniffing around."

He hurried off into the back of the house and returned with a white bag. You could smell what was inside it as soon as he entered the room.

"You: Go with him," Yoni told me. "Make sure he hides it and doesn't throw it out on the way home."

He scooped up the kid's backpack, which was lying on the floor, and took out the books and files that were in it. He put the white bag inside, then zipped the backpack up again.

"What is it?"

"What do you think?" asked Yoni. "Can't you smell it? Give it to El Meche when he asks for it, later today or tomorrow."

"Who?" asked the kid.

"This guy!" Yoni replied, pointing at me. "You want me to introduce you or what? Now get out, we're done here."

The kid stayed sitting in his seat. He gave Yoni a sidelong glance.

"What are you waiting for?" Yoni said.

"I need my school things," replied the boy.

"El Meche will give them to you when you give him the bag back," Yoni said.

The kid stood up and slung his backpack over his shoulder. Yoni pressed play again and, in the film, we heard someone cry out. It was the mother of the boy who talked to dead people: She'd just found him speaking an unknown language, his eyes rolled back in his head.

We went back out into the street; it looked like it was going to rain. It smelled of the dinner the woman in the house next door was cooking, and I hadn't even had lunch yet.

"Where am I going to put it?" the boy asked me while we walked.

"That's your problem," I said. "Didn't Yoni say there were lots of rooms in the inn?"

"But they're all occupied," the boy said.

"Well, put it in your room," I replied.

"My brother sleeps there, too," he said. "And my uncle—my uncle will realize."

"That's not my problem, kiddo," I told him.

We turned the corner and crossed to the middle of the street. His grandma's shop was on the other side, a shop that sold everything: food, drinks, toiletries.

"You'd better not let my grandma see you," he said.

I crossed the street and went into the store. An old woman was sitting behind the counter, watching a TV that stood next to her. She looked at me as if the devil himself had entered her store. I grabbed a couple of bags of potato chips and a few cans of soda while the boy said hello to his grandmother and apologized for being late. He really was a wimp. I left the shop without paying and I could hear the old woman shouting after me, but I just walked off.

The next day I didn't go and collect the white bag because things with the police had gotten complicated. Yoni said that some lookout had ratted on him. We all lay low for a few days, and then Yoni finally sent me to get the bag. I had to wait a while because the grandmother was in the shop and I couldn't see the kid anywhere. But when he didn't show up and it was starting to get dark, I had to go into the shop and speak to the old woman.

"Is Santiago here?" I said.

The grandmother pretended I didn't exist. She didn't reply or even look at me, just carried on watching the TV. I took out my piece and put it down on the counter, half blocking the TV so she'd pay attention. She turned around and walked over to a refrigerator in the back, reached up, and took down a bag from the top of it. She dumped it down on the counter, and I grabbed it and ran off to find Yoni.

"The kid wasn't there," I told him, handing over the bag. "But his grandmother gave it to me."

Yoni opened it up and counted the baggies inside.

"Do you want me to go and find him?" I asked him.

"He's already gone to the other side," he told me.

"To the Salvatrucha's turf?" I asked.

"The other side means the other side," he said. "They sent him to the United States."

THERE

SNA

OUT

ARE
KES
THERE

ALEJANDRO

THERE ARE SNAKES OUT THERE, IN THE DESERT, ON THE border at Sonoyta. We went up to the border but there were loads of federales, and immigration officers, and the sheer number of police spooked the guides, so they left us there, on the Mexican side. I had come with a cousin of mine who was a year older than me: I was fifteen, he was sixteen. My cousin told me we had to wait now, said we hadn't come all this way just to stay where we were. It wasn't just the fifteen of us who had left Guatemala together. There were more of us now, twenty or so—from Honduras, El Salvador, Mexico, even one from Ecuador.

The immigration agents knew we were migrants, obviously, because we were in the desert, on the border between Mexico and the United States. When they saw we were in Mexican territory they didn't say anything, just stared at us from a distance. You could see they weren't taking their eyes off us, and there were snakes there, too, in the way they stared.

We were in the mountains now, up on a hill looking out over the desert, and we had to stand around waiting, seeking out the shade of the few trees there were, or making shade with our own bodies. It was May or June, I don't really remember, and it was really hot, and the sun was strong, and we were burning. But the guides said we had to stay alert, we had to look and see if there was a chance to cross, a chance that Immigration might get distracted and then they could send us through. But time went by and nothing, just the heat and the sun that burned, and someone said that there were snakes out there, the dangerous ones, the ones that can come while you're asleep and sting you with their poison. It was someone who'd been over there already, someone who'd been sent back and who said that if Immigration caught you they put you in a cell where you never saw the sun, they gave you a cold burger to eat, and sometimes there was no space to lie down, you had to sleep sitting up.

My cousin kept saying to pay him no attention, that Immigration wasn't going to get us, that we hadn't come all this way—Chiapas, Hidalgo, Oaxaca, Guadalajara—just to stay here. Night fell, and we could see the lights of the cars over there, on the other side of the border, and someone said that, over there, there were no snakes. Over there, compared to our towns, it was completely different, really sophisticated. Now it was pitch black, and a hunger came over us, and we each took out what we'd brought to eat: tins of fish, of ham, canned hot dogs. And we had to eat just a little and ration it out, because we didn't know how long we would have to wait. The guides told us that they could take us back to the house where we'd been before we reached the border, but then they wouldn't be able to take us across.

After the night came down, I felt scared and sad, I felt so far away from my family, from my little brothers and my mom, and I felt bad for my dad, who is an alcoholic. He can't really take care of us. There are snakes there, too, in my dad's head. I couldn't sleep because I was worried. I had to stay alert to see if there was any chance of crossing and, besides, there were lots of sounds out in the desert, things crawling along that I thought were the snakes, those snakes that come and sting you with their poison if you fall asleep. And there were coyotes, too. We could see them in the distance, and they didn't come any closer, but some people said that if we listened we'd be able to hear them howling.

The night passed like that and then the day, and then another night, and my cousin said that we had to hold on, that if we'd held on this far we couldn't go back now, that we knew how difficult it was going to be to cross the desert, more difficult than the part on the train. In Oaxaca we had to sleep on the train for part of the journey, which is really dangerous. We were traveling up top, on the roof, for half a day and a night, risking falling off. They say lots of people have died coming north this way on the train. A few times we slept on the bus, too, and others we had to sleep by the sea, on the beach, and in

Chiapas we had to sleep by the river, and sometimes, like in Mexico City, we slept in a hotel. When we were in Mexico City I went out to buy something to eat and there was a group of people in the street—I think they were Zetas—and they were clashing with the police. There was a fight right there in the street, people with guns, with snakes in their heart.

And on the third day in the desert, on the border at Sonoyta, there were still loads of federales, lots of Immigration. At one point I found a snake—*we* found a snake, I mean, me and the people I was with, but luckily we managed to kill it. They told us it had the dangerous kind of venom that could kill you.

My cousin wasn't scared of the snakes and said that we hadn't escaped from the gangs back home just to be killed by some snake's poison. And I remembered that some of the guys in the gangs had tattoos of snakes, snakes on their arms, or on their backs, even on their heads or their bellies.

There was one guy who was in a gang who actually threatened to beat me up. It was at school, and he believed he was in charge because he was with this gang—and that's when I felt like I was in danger. And all for a silly little thing. I was talking to a girl in my class about an assignment, and he thought I was flirting with his girlfriend. And for that one silly little thing he wanted to take my life.

I had to change schools, but even then, there was a time when they came after me. When I got out of school they chased me and wanted to kill me. But I managed to escape; I ran off and got on one of the school buses that took me home. But I didn't feel safe anymore, I was afraid they might come around the corner and kill me at any minute. They had blades, knives, they could have had guns. I'd heard that they'd whacked other kids and that was when I started to worry that they might do something bad to me or my family, because back there anything can happen; it's not safe at all. The guys in these gangs can kill your whole family.

And all that running away just to end up in the desert, on the border at Sonoyta, with no way of crossing. I was already getting desperate, what with the days we'd spent in the desert, our skin all burned, unable to have a wash or anything proper to eat. I was getting desperate and I said that the best thing for it was to hand ourselves in, so we'd get sent back to our country.

There were about ten of us boys who wanted to hand ourselves in. Then the guides said that we could go back or do whatever we wanted, that it was in our hands, because they weren't going to take us over anymore. But one of the boys who'd crossed over before and been arrested said that we didn't know what a cell was like, those cells they call freezers. That for people like us who hadn't experienced it, being locked up like that, without seeing the sun, was really hard, and they treat you like a prisoner. And then I thought that I would prefer not to see the sun, because it was so hot in the desert and the sun was really strong, and I could handle being in the cell, since there are lots of people who come with little children, little kids who are brave enough to come this far. Crossing the desert is really difficult, but there are kids who come on their own and pregnant women about to give birth.

Five days went by in the desert, on the border at Sonoyta, and I told my cousin I couldn't take it any longer, that I really was going to hand myself in. We walked down the hill to where the Immigration agents were. To help take my mind off the snakes I thought about a memory from when I was really little. What I liked doing most of all was being a businessman and going to work with my dad. I used to go with him to sell things, when I was four years old, before I started school. He was a carpenter, and I helped him to sell his products. We'd leave the house and it'd be a nice day, sunny, but a normal sun, not like this sun that was burning me out here in the desert. He'd hold my hand and take me with him to see his customers, and what I loved most of all was just being with him.

We ten boys walked down the mountain and that's where I had to hand myself over to Immigration. We told them to send us back and that's how we handed ourselves over: We crossed the border and they were there, waiting for us. They put us in cars to take us to the freezers.

If I go back to my country, I feel something bad will happen to me.

IT WAS LIKE

BUT

TOUCHED IT

JUST

COTTON, WHEN I IT WAS ICE

DYLAN

Thursday, March 13, 2014

THE COUNSELOR TOLD ME THAT IF I LIKED READING I COULD write a diary about the days I spend here at the children's home in Chicago. She gave me a notebook and a blue pen and told me to write my name on the first page. My age. And where I was from. *So you don't lose it*, she said. *Or so if you do lose it, people will know whose it is, so they can return it to you.* She sat looking at me in silence, as if waiting for me to do something. I think she wanted to see if I really knew how to write. I opened the notebook and bent over the table. I wrote "Dylan" and my surname. "10 years old. Chalatenango, El Salvador." Then she said that I can show her what I wrote, or I can keep it just for me. I can write whatever I want to: how I feel, the things that happened to me, anything at all. This is because I told her I like reading about things in the past. History. But I don't know if I'm going to like writing about my own history.

They have a little library here with a few books in Spanish. I took out a book about the history of airplanes. Who invented them. The most important flights. Stuff like that. I also like books about sea creatures, but they don't have any of those here.

I'd never been on a plane until they took me out of the freezer and sent me here. In the freezer, at five in the morning, they called out our names and put us on some buses. Those buses were done out like we were in a film. Like we were prisoners from a maximum-security jail, with bars on the window and everything. The girls sat up front and the boys in the back.

They took us to the airport, put us on a plane, and brought us here. It was an immigration plane that only had migrant kids on it. Girls in front and boys in the back. It was the first time any of us had been on a plane. There were kids like me, ten years old, or nine or eight. And other older ones: eleven, fourteen—there were even some who looked sixteen or seventeen. When the plane took off we all screamed. Some with excitement and others with fear. Just like when we landed.

When I'm older, maybe I can be a pilot.

Saturday 15

Here in the home, every day is more or less the same. We get up, we wash, we have English classes, we eat breakfast, and they let us play soccer or basketball, or we watch films, we eat lunch, and the ones who are best behaved are allowed to play video games. I still haven't gotten to play any video games, though I don't know why. We can go out into the yard if we want, but it's cold, really cold. Even though they gave us all these thick overcoats. There are four beds in the room I sleep in. Every room has four beds. We also have to help make the beds and take the dirty washing to the laundry room.

Today I was allowed to speak to my mom on the phone. She told me not to worry, that she was going to send the papers they asked her for so that I could go live with her in Los Angeles. She said it would take a few days, because she had to get all the papers together and post them out. But she said to be calm, not to worry; she said it over and over. I know my mom's voice really well and I can tell she's worried. You could hear she was about to start crying. Her voice is the only thing I know really well. I've known my mom's voice since I was very little, but only her voice, because when she went to the United States I was only six months old. Maybe they'll let me go and live with her if they know that I've never met her. That I only know her voice. That's not normal.

In the afternoon, we played a game of soccer. The kids from El Salvador against the kids from Guatemala. We won 4–1. The Guatemalan kids are really bad.

Sunday 16

In the morning when I was getting dressed, some of the kids looked at me and saw my burns. They started asking what had happened to me. I didn't want to tell them, because I don't like being pitied. But they kept on asking until I had to tell them. It all happened at school, back home in Chalatenango. There were these kids who would beat me up, every day, and that's why I didn't like going to school. They were a year older than me. I don't know why they attacked me, they didn't say, they just did it. I'd go and tell the teacher and the teachers didn't care, they didn't do anything—it was a real problem. They beat up some friends of mine, too. Sometimes we'd say that we ought to defend ourselves, hit them back, but I didn't want to because I didn't want to end up getting more hurt. I was scared. I was really scared.

School was from seven in the morning until noon. At nine o'clock it was recess. And one day I was playing hide-and-seek at recess and when I went around the back of the school to look for a friend they were waiting for me. There were four of them. They had a hot piece of tubing with them. They'd gone to heat it up in one of their houses, one who lived near the school. It was a plastic tube, all melted. They grabbed me and held it to my hand. And then on my arm. And my back. I ran away, all the way home. My grandma cleaned my wounds and took me to the doctor. They gave me some cream to rub on. And this big dressing. My grandma was tired of me being beaten up; she said she was tired of them hurting me so much. That's why I came here.

Tuesday 18

I was talking to a bigger boy out in the yard, a kid from Guatemala. He must have been around fourteen, fifteen years old. We'd just had lunch and had gone outside to play, but we had to wait because there was a game going on between Mexico and Honduras.

The boy told me that he was in another home before this one, and in that one there were girls, too. He was laughing as he said it. But they had a rule in this other home that you always had to be at an arm's length away from people. Unless you were playing a game or eating lunch or something, you couldn't sit down with anyone close by because the caregiver would come by to check you weren't doing anything wrong. The boy said that there were kids who got together with other girls or boys right there in the home, and so they had this rule to avoid any problems. And he laughed again—I think he must have had a girlfriend there. I was going to ask him, but I was too embarrassed.

Friday 21

Today it was freezing, and nobody wanted to go out into the yard. Everyone wanted to stay inside and play. Or watch TV. Or play video games. Today and yesterday I got to play video games. Suddenly someone came running over and shouted for us to all go out into the yard, quick, to come and see what was happening. We all ran out. Outside there was snow falling. I took off my gloves and stretched out my hands and turned my face up to the sky. I thought it would be like cotton, but when I touched it, it was just ice.

Saturday 22

In the morning we played by throwing snowballs at each other. It wasn't snowing anymore, but lots of snow had fallen and it was so cold that it wouldn't melt. If you kept your gloves on, they would get wet. If you took them off, the snow was so cold it made your hands hurt. It almost felt like the snow was burning.

Monday 24

Nobody's telling me anything and I don't know how long I'll have to stay here. There are kids who've been here a long time—

two months, eight months, some even a whole year. Those kids get sad and everyone else tries to cheer them up, says there's still a chance they'll get out of here. And they try to cheer up every person who does get out, telling them it's going to turn out really well for them. I don't know if they'll send me to live with my mom in Los Angeles or send me back to my grandma in El Salvador. But my grandma can't take care of me anymore, because my grandpa is seriously ill and in the hospital. That's what my grandma told me, and she said I had to go.

They put me on a truck and I didn't know where I was going. The truck took us to Guatemala, thirteen of us. There were adults and kids with their relatives. From Guatemala they took us to Mexico on a bus. They didn't give us any food, but I wasn't hungry because I was worried about what was happening. I was scared. I was scared because I didn't know what was happening and I didn't know where we were. My grandma didn't really explain anything to me. I just overheard her say when she was talking to someone that she was praying to God that I wouldn't have to walk through the desert. And praying that the Zetas didn't catch me in Mexico, because when the Zetas catch kids you had to get money together to pay them off.

Once we were in Mexico they made us change buses to go to Monterrey. The bus didn't stop the whole way to Monterrey.

Then they took us to a house, but the house was full of mosquitos. There were more people there, more migrants. In the house, the men slept in the living room, on mattresses on the floor, and the women slept in the bedrooms. They gave us sandwiches and burritos to eat. One day Immigration came, and we had to hide. I had to hide in one of the bedrooms. The guy who opened the door told them there was nobody in there and they left.

Then they took us in a taxi to another house, a little house this time. Then they took us to the river in another truck. There were about seventeen of us in the trucks going to the river. We crossed over on a raft, a rowboat. They only had two boats to get people across, and there were about seven people in each boat. I was in the second group to go across. It was raining, kind of drizzling. It was nighttime. We walked for about half an hour until some trucks pulled up. Immigration caught us. They caught all of us.

They took us to an immigration center and locked us up in a freezer. It was just boys, although there were only four the same age as me. I spoke with an agent there. I only told them my name, but they searched my things and in my backpack my grandma had put a piece of paper with my mom's phone number on it, and an aunt's who also lives in the United States. I was in the freezer for three days.

Tuesday 25

The counselor told me what I'd written was really good. Said it was great that I'd written about the burns and about the time those other kids had beaten me up. That I was very brave for doing that. She asked me if I wanted to tell her anything else about it. That sometimes talking can make you feel better. I told her that they also used to hassle me outside school. The kids from the gangs. There were a few of them. Tall. They carried knives. They told me that if I didn't join them by the time I was ten they'd kill me. And my friends. They'd say this to us in the street, after school. We were scared. We would run away to keep safe. My cousin had to change schools because there were boys hassling her.

My grandma said that the gangs had destroyed the country, that they've turned everything upside down. That people were abandoning villages, whole towns, leaving their crops and their animals behind to go somewhere else. And that people aren't brave enough to talk about what's happening in their communities. And that's why I had to leave. Even though it was really dangerous. But, like they say, nothing ventured, nothing gained.

Wednesday 26

The counselor told me that my case has been approved. That in a few days I could go and be with my mom, that they were going to put me on a plane to go be with her.

(We lost at soccer to the kids from Honduras. But we won against Mexico on penalties.)

Friday 28

I was woken early in the morning and told to get up and have a shower. Then they put me on a truck and took me on a train to the airport in Chicago. There were seven of us kids traveling together. At the airport we said goodbye to some of the others. Two who were going to New York and another one who was going to Carolina. The other four of us were going to Los Angeles. The flight was going to leave at seven thirty in the morning, but it was delayed and we just sat there. So while we were waiting, the person who was accompanying us called my mom to tell her about the delay and that she would have to pick me up at the airport later than we thought. It took us about three hours to get there—to me it felt like ages. But it was really cool getting onto the plane. When we arrived, I ran to the pick-up area, and that was when I saw my little brother, and my mom recognized me.

I just hugged her. I hugged her. I hugged her hard because I didn't recognize her. I'd thought she was going to be taller.

My stepdad drove us from the airport to the house where we were going to live. Or where I was going to live from now on, because they all lived there already. My mom and my stepdad parked the car outside a really big building and said that we had arrived. "Wow," I said, "my mom has this whole building?" All three of them burst out laughing. You say the funniest things, Dylan, said my mom.

They just live in one of the apartments.

I'D
DIE
TO GET

RATHER TRYING OUT

NICOLE
AND KEVIN

THE LIGHTS TURNED RED, AND THE MAN IN THE TRUCK stopped to look at his phone. His head was bowed, his neck sore from having repeated this gesture over and over again throughout the day. It was nearing seven p.m. now, and it was dark already.

The gentle tapping at the window brought him back to reality; he was third in the line of cars at the traffic light. He thought that someone had washed his windshield without him noticing and was now asking him for money. *Damn it.* But no: His windshield was as filthy as ever. More tapping at the window. He looked: It was two little kids, a girl and a boy. Automatically, without thinking about it, he signaled no, that he wasn't going to give them any money, and turned back to his phone.

The light was still red and not two seconds passed before he heard the tapping again. He lowered the window, on the verge of losing his temper.

"Can you give us a lift?" said the girl, who was younger than the boy. "We can go in the back, in the trailer."

He looked at them as the light went green. They didn't look like street kids: They were dirty, their clothes pretty ragged, but they didn't have that look of utter bleakness like children who have realized they have no future. There was still hope in their faces. The boy, who he guessed was around fifteen, sixteen at most, had his left arm in a cast. The girl couldn't have been more than ten years old. He heard the desperate honking of the cars lining up behind him and looked at the space that had opened up between his truck and the intersection ahead.

"Where are you headed?" he asked.

"To the border," replied the girl who, although younger, seemed to be the more talkative of the two—perhaps she had faith in her ability to generate pity; perhaps this was the strategy they used to get help.

"That's a really long way away," the man said, "over six hundred miles."

"Do you know a bus or something that would take us there?" the boy asked.

The car behind switched its headlights into full beam and began honking the horn in a frenzy.

"People are so rude," said the man.

Suddenly he opened the door, the children stepped back to let him pass, and he walked over to where the other driver behind him was gesticulating, demanding he move his truck. The man leaned down toward the window of the other driver, an older man who looked like a civil servant or a university professor.

"Can't you see I'm busy?" he said.

"You're in the way, buddy," the other man said. But he regretted his words before he'd even finished the sentence, because he saw a gun peeping out from inside the truck man's jacket.

"Is there a problem?" asked the truck driver, glancing quickly down inside his jacket.

The other guy cranked his car into gear and began to switch lanes.

"Not at all," he said, "sorry to bother you."

The man walked back to his truck. The kids were still standing there, waiting for him.

"Let's go," he told them, "I'll give you a ride."

"Where to?" said the boy.

"Get in," he said. "You want a ride or not?"

The girl walked around the truck without checking with her brother, frightened the man would change his mind. They had been walking all day, and the prospect of sitting down while covering several miles, whichever direction it was in, seemed to her like a wonderful idea.

"Hang on," the boy said.

The girl ignored him, and so he was obliged to follow her. When she opened the door, the boy pushed past her, trying to get in first.

"Excuse me, sir: ladies first," said the man with the truck.

The boy sat down in the middle, next to the man, and the girl shut the door.

"Ladies first, I said," said the man.

The boy didn't move.

"Get out, in that case," said the man, threateningly.

The girl clambered over her brother, giving him a push so he would sit down by the door.

"That's better," said the man. "I'm doing you a favor so the least you can do is be grateful."

The lights had gone red again, but the man accelerated to cross the intersection. Two cars had to brake hard to avoid a crash.

"You went through a red light," the boy said.

"Thanks for the advice," replied the man.

He took a right on the next street, heading toward the outskirts of town.

"Did you come on your own, no coyote?" he asked.

"We didn't have any money," said the girl. "We didn't have enough."

"What's your name?" he asked her.

"Nicole," she said.

"And you?" he asked the boy.

"My brother's name is Kevin," said Nicole.

"From El Salvador?"

"No, Guatemala," said Nicole.

"And how did you get this far?" he asked.

Once again, it was Nicole who answered:

"One day my brother said to me, *Nicole, do you want to go and see Mom?* I said I did. So he said I had to start saving money. And we did, only we didn't have enough, and our money ran out."

"We got here on trucks and buses with the money we'd saved," said Kevin.

"And where's your mom?" asked the man.

"Los Angeles," replied Nicole.

The man was driving confidently through a tangle of streets in what looked like an industrial park: factories, warehouses, vacant lots, gas stations with dozens of trucks and trailers parked out front.

"What's it called here?" Nicole asked.

"What?" said the man.

"You know," she insisted, "the city where we are."

"You don't know where we are?" said the man.

The kids were silent.

"So how are you going to get to the border, then?"

"We ask people and sometimes they help us," said Nicole. "Sometimes they ask us if we're hungry and give us burritos. Or sometimes tacos."

"What happened to your arm?" the man asked the boy.

Kevin ran his right hand over his cast but said nothing.

"What's the matter?" asked the man. "Cat got your tongue?"

"The guys from the gang back in Guatemala broke it, the mareros," said Nicole. "They beat him up on the street when he was on his way back from playing baseball. They were trying to force him to join the gang and he said no so they broke his arm."

"And who did you live with back in Guatemala?" the man asked.

"My aunt," said Nicole. "First, we lived with my grandma, when my mom went to the United States, but then the mareros killed her because she refused to pay the rent they were charging us. We owned a few shops and so the mareros thought we had money. They go after any business they think has money, they go after stores, anyone who works, and they ask them for money. My mom says that they attack families to get their revenge, and they wanted to kill us all because she'd run away. She sent us money from the U.S. and my grandmother had to give some of this money to the mareros. My mom was basically working to pay them off, and one day my grandma just got tired of it all and stopped paying, and so they killed her. And they killed my uncle, too. That's why we decided to come here—Kevin used to say he'd rather die in Mexico than get killed in Guatemala. *Nicole*, he'd say to me, *I'd rather die trying to get out.*"

Kevin kicked Nicole's foot; he hadn't elbowed her earlier to get her to shut up because he would have hurt his arm.

"What?" Nicole said.

They left the industrial park and got onto a highway. Kevin caught a glimpse of a sign that read "Zacatecas 110 miles."

"Where are we going?" Nicole asked again.

The man turned on the radio.

"You like music?" he asked the girl.

She replied that she did, that she loved it.

"Pick a station," the man told her.

She tuned to the third station, where they played música norteña, but then turned the dial again until she found a song in English. The highway was deserted; other vehicles went past only every now and then, their headlights shining into the truck's cab. There was nothing around them, except for the odd tire repair shop or the remnants of an abandoned gas station and darkness. The man drove skillfully, avoiding the potholes, as if he knew the way by heart.

"Does your mom know you're out here?" he asked.

"No," Nicole said. "If we told her she wouldn't have let us come. She says that crossing Mexico is really dangerous, she had a really hard time getting across Mexico, and she doesn't

want us to have a hard time as well or to come over by ourselves. When we told her we wanted to go across to be with her
she said she'd rather come back to Guatemala. But she can't
come back, because if she does they'll kill her."

"So you ran away, basically," said the man.

"One day my brother told me that we were going to ask my
aunt for permission to take a trip and that's how we were going
to get away," said Nicole. "I said, *What if she doesn't believe us,
Kevin?* But Kevin said our aunt would, because we were going
to do it when there really was a school trip. We were going to ask
her permission for this trip, but really, we were going to come
here. And that's what we did, and on the day of the trip, we
came here instead with all the money we'd saved up, but now
it's all gone."

The man took his foot off the accelerator, pressed down
lightly on the brake and steered the truck toward the side of
the road. Out of the utter darkness, a strip of very fine earth
appeared, like talcum powder, all dusty. The truck tires immediately raised a cloud that surrounded everything. The road
here was unpaved and on some stretches the truck had to force
its way through the bushes and acacia trees.

"Where are we going?" Kevin asked again.

"This way's quicker," the man replied.

He gripped the wheel hard, pressed down on the accelerator, and the truck sped off into the Mexican night.

HE AND

ALONG

WE

I GOT
REALLY
LL

MIGUEL ÁNGEL

— Did you see how they're looking at us?
— They must suspect something.

BACK ON MY ISLAND, ALL I DID WAS GO FROM SCHOOL TO
home and from home back to school again, and then I made a
decision: that when I finished ninth grade I'd immigrate to the
United States. I lived with my grandmother, an uncle (my
father's brother), and my big sister.

My mom is from Honduras and my dad is from El Salvador, but, when I was fourteen, my mom left us and decided to
make her life with someone else. She went back to her country
and left us on our own, and then my grandmother died, and
we were even more alone.

My dad went to the U.S. in 2007, because of the situation
with work, so he could provide for us—he had to go to give us
a better life. He always looked out for me and my sister. And
my mom, too, until she decided to go and live with someone
else.

— What's your name?
— César. What's yours?
— Miguel Ángel.

On the island where I lived everyone knew one another. It's a small place, with about five hundred people living there, and everyone says hello and talks to one another when they go out into the fields, or to the beach. When I was there, the kids who used to be my friends would show me their fists, saying they were going to punch me, but I would try and move away. They'd shout at me in the street and say I was someone who shouldn't exist. They showed me their fists, but I tried to avoid them, so it didn't get any more serious than that.

— *It's better they don't know.*
— *But they're not discriminating against us.*
— *It's still better they don't know.*

I realized when I was fourteen years old. When my mom abandoned me and my sister, I felt more alone, and when I felt alone I needed someone who would show me affection. That's when I realized I was gay.

— *How old are you?*
— *Nineteen. You?*
— *Sixteen.*

I went to school from Monday to Friday. Sometimes on Saturdays I went to watch the other kids play, but when I did, my old friends were always around and implying things, saying stuff like *Here comes the faggot* and laughing at me for my sexual orientation. By that point I'd stopped hanging out with them. If they were saying things like that then they weren't my friends anymore; they didn't have anything to do with friendship, because someone who treats another person badly is not a friend.

I felt good about myself and I still do. I never had a problem with it; I accept myself for how I am. But when other people hassled me, it affected me, because it hurt my dignity.

– Aren't you afraid something might happen to you?
– I'm afraid of Mexico; it's the most dangerous country in
  the world because of all the cartels and things.

Things were going well for me at school because I was getting good grades, but, on the other hand, they weren't going so well because the other kids would bother me because of my identity. They'd shout rude things at me: When we played basketball, they'd say it was a game for faggots, and that soccer was for real men, but basketball wasn't.

This all started when they saw me talking to a kid who was my boyfriend, and then they started to suspect that there was something going on between us, even though we weren't doing anything, we weren't kissing or anything like that. But they suspected we had something between us and that we were going out with each other. And then they said horrible things to me, they shouted that word at me in the street. They always treated me that way.

   — Why did you decide to come here?
   — Because back where I used to live you can't be the way
     I am.

I used to go to a beach on my own, where not many people go; it's a solitary kind of beach. I would go just to walk around, because I wasn't hanging out with anyone, for the same reasons—because they all treated me badly. I didn't go to the beach with my family because things weren't good with them, either. My family would hear rumors and they all started to distance themselves from me. I wasn't getting any support or protection from my friends or my family.

My family suspected that I was gay and they started saying awful things to me. My sister would say to my uncle that I might have a boyfriend and my uncle believed everything she said and started shouting at me, saying awful things. He said that he didn't want a faggot in his house.

   — So, where you do want to get to?
   — New York, where my dad is.

— Does he know . . . ?

*— No, I haven't told him because I don't know what would
happen.*

There was one day when I was studying in the city, because on
the island you couldn't study for your high school diploma, so
on Wednesdays and Fridays I had to go across to the mainland
to do a virtual diploma—back then there weren't any computers
on the island. In the city some bad people threatened me on my
way to class. They noticed me in the street and told me they
didn't want to see me around there again, because they'd do
something to me. I'm sure they figured out my sexual orientation. In my country no one accepts gay people.

In the city there are lots of gangs, the Mara Salvatrucha and
the M-18, all looking to see who wants to take part in doing
bad stuff. And if you refuse, they say that they're going to kill
you. Or they don't even tell you, they just go and do it. Or else
they demand rent off you.

If you're gay they bother you even more. Gay people they
rape and kill.

— Do you think it won't be the same over there?

*— I think it'll be different. I don't want to be discriminated
against, because the whole time on the island people
would shout at me, whistle at me, treat me badly, and*

make me feel so low.

— Hopefully it won't be like that over there.

— I'm sure they won't treat me like that.

I told my dad that I wanted to go to the United States with him, but I didn't tell him the reason. My dad doesn't know, and he wouldn't accept it if I said to him, "Dad, I'm gay." Because he doesn't love people like that, either; he's kind of against gay people. I never told him I was gay because I didn't know what would happen.

My dad always looked out for me, he sent us money, but he's never known about this thing with my sexual orientation. My uncle didn't tell him anything, but he did have an idea that I was gay.

— Do you feel something like that for me?

When I was in the States one of my cousins started sending me messages, saying that he didn't like me because I was gay, and then he told me if I was deported something would happen to me, because he's in a gang. I was really scared, I still am scared, scared that if I go back he'll do something bad to me. He's in the 18th Street gang, and so I'm scared he might do something to me.

– If I'd stayed it would have been risky. I'd have been at
school and it would have been dangerous.
– What would you like to study?
– I want to study journalism.

On the way here, I met someone from my country, called César. We got along really well. He and I had things in common. I really liked him, and he really liked me.

We made the journey with ten people, eight men and two women, including a six-year-old boy traveling with his mom. They saw us and they were laughing and they kind of suspected something, but they didn't discriminate, they weren't bothering me. They were respectful.

He and I still talk sometimes, but he's in California. And when we talk, there are times when we actually get into those topics. I ask him if he ever thinks about me, and he tells me that he does.

We both know it's something we'll always remember.

– Do you ever think about me?
– Yes, I do.

HOW

WERE GOING

THE

WE
TO GET
RE

SANTIAGO AND DANIEL

SAYING GOODBYE

On the morning of the day we left, my brother and I got up really early. We went to church, because we always go to church, and the priest was a good friend of ours. We went so he could give us his blessing, and to ask him to pray for us. I was a little bit scared, scared that something might happen to me on the way. Mexico was what I was most scared of. The cartels and things, stuff like that. Before we left, one of my friend's cousins had gone and the journey had taken him around two months, because he was in the city of the Zetas, and the cartels were really powerful, and so the coyotes had to hide them in a house somewhere for a really long time. That's why we wanted to go and see the priest, but he was saying Mass and so we just gave him the message that we were leaving now and asked him to pray for us.

Then, since my uncle has a car, he drove us to the border. We left at eight in the morning and we reached the border around ten. At ten we stopped at the exact place we'd been told. A bus stopped there that took you directly to the border with Guatemala, because we weren't right on the border, not exactly. We all said goodbye to one another there, to my uncle, my grandmother, my other aunt, my uncle's wife, and our little cousin, because they'd all come to see us off. And I had my little cousin on my lap and she didn't want me to go. All I told her was: *Wait here, I'm just going to buy some pupusas.*

YOU'RE NOT STAYING HERE

They told us to get on this bus and get off at the last stop and that there'd be some people waiting for us there. And then we got on the bus, just the two of us, we waited until the last stop, still in El Salvador, and when we got off there were two people on bikes waiting for us. Then we walked. They went ahead of us and we walked behind them, five yards or so behind. Then one of them stopped and waited for us to catch up and he asked for all the money we were carrying. He told us he was going to take it someplace with him for safekeeping. So we did. Then the other guy led us to a place on the river, on the border with Guatemala. He said we were going to cross the river and I thought we'd do it in a boat or something, but no, we had to walk across. The water came halfway up my body, and nearly as high on my brother because we're practically the same height. We had to take off our pants, our shoes; we went across wearing just our boxer shorts and T-shirts. We were alone, alone, all alone, at that part of the river. It was just us and the guy who was with us. There were some men taking sand out of the river, but they didn't say anything to us.

We walked across, and the current was quite strong and the rocks at the bottom were really slippery, and so I was walking really carefully, and my brother started to slip. And so I said to him: *No, come on, you're not staying here.* And we pulled him out. Then we finally got to the other side, the Guatemalan side. We put our clothes back on, put everything on, but we'd taken less than five steps, not even two steps just to get into Guatemala, and already there was a Guatemalan waiting for us with a balaclava and a knife. He told us to give him everything we had. We didn't hear him properly, and so the guy who was with us said: *I'm from here, man, from here, so we've got a problem.* I didn't really understand him, because he spoke so fast. In the end our guide just gave the other guy twenty dollars and we carried on.

We walked for about fifteen minutes and got to a dirt road and the other guide, the one we'd split from before, was there waiting for us. He told us that the money we'd given him had been stolen, that another Guatemalan guy had jumped him, too, on the other road, and that he'd had to hand over the money.

After that we got onto the bus that was going to take us to the main terminal in Guatemala and we were on it from about eleven o'clock to seven in the evening.

And then we got to the capital.

ALL THE PEOPLE WHO ARE GOING TO CROSS OVER

We waited there until midnight. We got together with two other people who were making the journey. A girl and her boyfriend. Then we all left on the bus around midnight, heading for the Mexican border. We got to the final bus stop at six a.m., and there was a car waiting for us. We were taken to a hotel and from there we got a minibus, which took us to a place with lots of hotels next to a river, and that's where all the people who are going to cross over come. They're not exactly hotels; they're like houses with a communal dining room added on. All the people who are going to cross over meet there, eat, and wait for a while, and then a group sets off. Then another group arrives and sets off.

We got there at around eight in the morning. We waited a while, they gave us something to eat, and we set off at ten.

THERE WERE CROCODILES THERE

We got into a boat to cross the river and get to Mexico. There were about twenty people and there was water coming into the boat. It took us two and a half hours to get from one side to the other. We didn't go straight across, partly because there were crocodiles there, and partly because there were more checkpoints as well. Some people had passed through earlier, and they'd gone to see if there were any checkpoints. There were rapids in this river, and so they told us to all get in the back of the boat but then the bow rose up. It was being tossed around all over the place and we all just shouted, *Ay ay ay ay ay.* We got really seasick. We were scared because it was the first time we'd been on a boat and seen crocodiles. There were about five on one side, another five close by, and some people were acting like it was just a day out: *Oh, look, there's one, there's another one, there's a monkey.*

We arrived at a place to get fuel, but we didn't stop, we just drifted past slowly and they handed over the fuel—one of the guys steering the boat had to get out to reach the gas, and he almost got eaten by a crocodile, but we all yelled and threw a rock at it. It didn't get him; the captain escaped. After this we finally reached the place where we had to get off.

QUICKLY AND QUIETLY

We walked inland for about fifteen minutes, maybe more. Now we were in Mexico. My brother and I were pretty scared. We got to some houses where there were a few cars waiting for us, cars with these raised covers on the back, pickups, really. The coyotes sent us over and we all got in and sat down, so the covering would hide us and no one would be able to tell there was anyone in the back of the cars. Then they took us to a house made out of wooden posts and cement. Five people lived there; they gave us food, and we slept. It was pretty cold. They were indigenous people—only one of them spoke Spanish. One out of the five. The girl's boyfriend and I slept on the floor. They gave my brother a hammock and he slept there with the girl. We had sweaters with us, but it was still really cold.

We set off again at three in the morning, in the trucks with the coverings like before, and we were quiet, really quiet. There were three pickups. In one there were twenty people, in another twenty more, and in the last one, fifteen. We were in the one with fifteen people, sitting down, practically lying, so you couldn't see us from outside the truck. We spent around three or four hours in there. At one point they made us get out because there was a roadblock up ahead, and we had to get out and walk around it. That took about ten minutes, moving really quickly. Quickly and quietly. Quickly and quietly. No one spoke. And if they did speak the others hushed them, saying: *They'll catch us, they'll catch us.*

We got back into the pickups and then we reached a place where we got on a bus. It was in a village, I don't know where, I forget the names. We got on this bus to go to another village and the coyotes were waiting for us there in another truck, and then they took us to another house.

THERE'D BE A MOMENT

In the house, they fed us, we rested for a while, we washed, and, after that, later on, like around six in the evening, the man who was traveling with us explained how we were going to get to Mexico City. He said that a bus would come by and we were to get into the luggage compartment, down below. So we went with him in the car and, when the bus got to the bus stop, we all sort of gathered around it, and then the girl and her boy-friend got in first, then the man, my brother, and then me—I was the last. There were five of us in that space. I was right by the door. The man who made us get in the luggage compart-ment told us that there would be a moment when the air con-ditioning would be switched off. Every compartment had air conditioning, in case they're carrying something that might melt, that sort of thing. And he said that when the air condi-tioning and the lights went off, it'd be because we were in the terminal where they pick up passengers, and that we couldn't speak at all at that point, not one little bit. And there near the door, right where I was, was a telephone for speaking to the driver, and he'd let me know when it was time to get off.

The bus made a stop, and we were quiet, not making any noise. I felt like I was suffocating; I'm scared of small spaces, I needed air. We stopped there for ten to fifteen minutes. After that, the bus drove on and on. For about two and a half hours, maybe three. We tried to sleep, but it was impossible. And so we talked about what was going to happen, about how we were going to cross the border. That was when we all got to know one another really well. Then the driver spoke to us and said he was going to make a stop, that he was going to stop for just five minutes and that was when we had to get off. He stopped, the guy who was in charge of opening the door got out and pulled back the curtains, and we got off. We moved away really quickly and went over to the car that was waiting for us, just like that.

Now we were in Mexico City.

THEN THEY STARTED PUTTING MORE AND MORE PEOPLE IN

They told us to put on our coats because it was about to get really cold. There was another car waiting to take us to another house, and we spent three days in that house, because there were Immigration agents all over the place. Since I know how to cook, I made us all chicken soup. We actually got to sleep in a bed in that place, and we had a bath.

On the third day, they came with a car for us and told us they were going to take us to Monterrey in a freight truck. The car came and picked us up, and then we swapped to another car in the middle of the highway. This car took us to another house where we waited and then got into the freight truck, in the front cab. We were there for around two hours. We were comfortable, more or less, but then they started putting more and more people in, more and more and more, into the front of the truck. After this they made us get into another truck, in the back this time.

Then there were more of us: At first there were around fifty or sixty people, all in the back of the truck; you could lie down in there, you could sit. The trailer had a few pieces of furniture in it. We were comfortable, we could move around freely. And then later the trailer stopped, and they put like twenty more people in and then another stop, another twenty people. And so on. There ended up being about a hundred and fifty people in total. We were all kind of crouched down, we could hardly breathe; I couldn't breathe.

There was one time when I couldn't bear squatting down any longer because I was really squashed, and so I stood up and I told my brother to lie down where I'd been so that he could rest. I stayed standing, and because of the heat coming off us and creating steam, the roof was dripping, and then the cold from outside made all these freezing droplets fall onto us. I was trying to sort my head out so I could sleep, and these little drops kept waking me up.

Next to us were some big Mexican guys who were talking

nonstop, using up all the oxygen, and everyone else thought that we were the ones talking, and they'd say to us: *Be quiet, be quiet.*

We'd been told that there'd be a time when the trailer would stop, and the driver would rev the engine twice, and that meant it was about to go past a checkpoint. And that when it only revved once, that was because there were police outside who had stopped us.

We spent twelve hours or longer in that trailer. I kept looking at the time on my phone. Then people started getting off, and one by one, bit by bit, they left, and when there was almost no one left in the back, they moved us up into the front again. We were the last ones to get off, and they dropped us at a gas station.

By then we were in Monterrey.

PRETEND YOU'RE ASLEEP

After that, a car picked us up and took us to a house, where there was another car that took us to a special bus stop with buses that would take us from Monterrey to Reynosa. The man there told us, "Listen, when you've been driving for an hour, an hour and a half, the bus will make a stop, and you'll go past some kind of checkpoint." When he said this, I got scared. But he told us that it might be closed, and that if for whatever reason it was open, we were to pretend to be asleep and nothing would happen.

Then, sure enough, after we'd been traveling for around two hours we went past a place with an immigration checkpoint, but it was closed. But half an hour later, a little farther on, we were stopped by some soldiers. We'd been told to pretend we were asleep if we were stopped by soldiers, too. They stopped the truck and my brother actually was asleep, he didn't have to pretend. Then they said, "Anyone with luggage down below, get off, we're going to check your bags." Since we didn't have anything, we didn't get off. We pretended to be asleep, and they shone their flashlights in on us to take a look but said nothing.

And we carried on, arriving in the city of Reynosa in the morning, where there was another car waiting to take us to the bodega. That's what they call it: the bodega.

SOFTLY, SOFTLY

Once we were at the bodega, we were five blocks or so from the river. There were quite a few people there. More and more kept arriving, then others would leave, and more would arrive, and we all slept on the floor. There, when they told you to make a line for the food, you had to run, grab your plate, wash it and then eat, because otherwise you wouldn't eat at all.

Every day, there were two attempts to cross: one in the

morning, really early, and another at night. We spent three days there, in the bodega. They were waiting for more people, because we were all going to hand ourselves in to Immigration. We had to, because if you didn't then you had to walk for ages through the desert, and I have health problems: Apart from being overweight, my heart is bigger than normal, and I get tired really easily, so I might not be able to handle walking for hours in the desert.

In the morning there was a group of the people who were going to hand themselves in to Immigration, and in the group, there were four little boys, a five-year-old girl, and another little boy who was with his father. They all left at around dawn, but they went via a part of the river that's not as deep, although the current is faster. They were walking across the river, and the current dragged the little girl away. She was holding on to an adult's hand, but she slipped away, the river just took her. She was just a little girl, five years old, from Honduras.

Then the head guy appeared, and he asked us, "Which of you are going to hand yourselves in? Put your hands up." And then he told us we'd have to wait one more day, because we had to wait for another group to arrive.

On the third day, at nighttime, we left. In our group was a mother with a little baby, two kids aged eight and seven from Guatemala who spoke Quiché, and a father with his daughter.

We walked to a spot where there was an inflatable boat. They blew it up and put it in the water. The guy who was going to steer got in first and went up to the front. Then the rest of us got in. Me, my brother, a woman who was helping out, the two little kids, and finally the dad with his little girl.

We moved forward softly, softly, rowing really quietly, because they'd told us there were crocodiles here, too. I don't know if it was true; I didn't see anything. They were rowing quietly so as not to make any noise, because Immigration might show up there, too.

We got to the other side of the river, climbed up onto the bank, and waited fifteen minutes for Immigration to get there. Two men on a quad bike arrived, and we went off with them, on foot.

I was carrying a little piece of paper, part of a label from a packet of medicine, and on it I'd written down my mom's cell phone number and her work number, so they could let her know I was here.

KAYLA

Cabuya

   a : fiber from the agave plant used to make rope
       and cloth
   b : rope, and especially that made from agave

IN FRONT OF US IS THE RIVER, THE WATER THAT RUNS SO
fast, like a bad-tempered person, someone really angry, really
mad. Everyone's scared, and some of them start trying to orga-
nize the others, telling them who should cross first and who
should cross next. They ask us if we know how to swim. I say,
"sort of," because I used to swim in the sea occasionally back
home in my village, in Pueblo Cortés. My cousin is more worried for her daughter. She holds her tightly to her chest and
starts rocking her to soothe her, but I think she's making her
more nervous. The baby cries and cries. She's probably tired or
hungry.

   "How old is the little girl?" asks a man with a flashlight. He
is from Honduras.

   "Eight months," my cousin replies.

   "Are you here on your own?" he says.

   "Just with my cousin," she replies, indicating me with a
flick of her chin.

   "And the girl's father?" he asks.

"In Honduras," says my cousin. "He wouldn't step up, he's never cared about her."

From a way off we can hear the cries of the people crossing the river. A girl who couldn't cross because she wasn't very strong starts to shout. Even though it's dark, we catch a glimpse of her by the light of the moon. She's gripping on tightly to the cabuya but she's sinking because she's thrashing around so much.

"Ay ay ay ay ay ay!" cries the girl.

She cries out that she's drowning and everyone else gets scared, and soon lots of people are shouting. Some are shouting from fear and others are shouting to try to calm the others down. Some people are shouting that if they don't stop shouting, Immigration is going to hear them. Some people on the banks, when they see the people in the river shouting, start to cry.

"I don't want to die, I don't want to die," says a boy who's soaking wet, who had changed his mind after he first got into the river and come back to the shore.

"Let God be the one who lets us cross safely," an older woman says, trying to calm him.

"The water's freezing," says the little boy. "It's so cold, so cold," he says over and over.

In the middle of the river two men grab hold of the girl and help her so she doesn't drown. Slowly, she calms down, and everyone stops shouting.

"If you hold on tight to the cabuya nothing will happen," the man says to my cousin.

"How am I supposed to hold on if I'm carrying my baby?" she replies.

The man thinks for a minute. Someone else says to switch off the flashlights, that we have to save the batteries for when we're on the other side of the river. We're plunged even further into darkness, but once you get used to the light from the moon you can just about see.

"How old are you?" the man asks me.

"Thirteen," I say, "almost fourteen."

He thinks again, as if working out how strong I am, and then goes over to speak to the other men. My cousin starts crying and says, "Don't cry, don't cry," to her baby.

"Put her on your breast, my child," an old woman tells her.

"She doesn't breastfeed," I tell her. "She gives the baby formula, but we've run out."

The woman ignores me.

"Put her on your breast," she says again. "That will calm her down."

"I don't have any milk!" my cousin says through tears. "The

doctor told me to give her formula because my milk wasn't coming in and the baby was getting hungry."

The man returns with another guy, a Mexican.

"Who have you two come with?" the Mexican asks.

"We're on our own," says my cousin.

"You didn't come with a guide?" he says.

We tell him we didn't.

"And how did you get here?" asks the man from Honduras.

"Well, like everyone does," I say. "On the train."

"And where are you going?"

"New York," says my cousin, trying not to cry.

"We have an aunt there," I say. "One of my dad's sisters."

"And how are you going to get all that way?" the Mexican asks. "You know it's really far away, don't you?"

"Well, like everyone does," I tell him, because I have no idea.

The Mexican looks at his watch.

"What time is it?" I ask him.

"Almost three."

The two men leave again to speak to the group trying to sort out all the chaos.

"I feel like I'm going to die," says my cousin, holding on to her little girl, who won't stop crying.

I don't say a thing, because I feel like I'm going to die, too.

I hear the river in the darkness rushing along, really loudly, like a really angry, evil person. Off in the distance you can't see the people crossing over anymore; they must have reached the other side by now. I hope that the river hasn't carried them off.

"Give the girl the breast, my child," the old woman says again to my cousin. "Even if you don't have any milk, it'll soothe her."

My cousin does as she says, but the baby won't latch on. I think she's out of the habit now, since my cousin hardly ever breastfeeds her.

"How old are you?" the woman asks my cousin.

"Sixteen."

"And you came here on your own?" the woman asks.

"Yes," replies my cousin. "Just the three of us."

"Do your parents know you're here?"

"No," I tell her. "We just left."

"So you ran away," says the old woman.

"Pretty much," says my cousin. "My dad died. I lived with my mom and she never has any work. Sometimes she takes in laundry. It's a really hard situation. I want my daughter to have a better future."

"And you?" the woman says to me. "What do your parents do?"

"Nothing," I tell her.

"Nothing? What do you mean, *nothing*?"

"Well," I say. "My dad's a musician, he plays guitar, but he doesn't have anything stable. Sometimes he gets paid for playing at a party, or in a bar, and we wait for him to get home so we can eat. Sometimes he doesn't come back. Or he does, but he doesn't bring anything. Sometimes we don't have anything to eat."

"What kind of music does he play?"

"He plays punta," I say.

"Is he good?" she asks.

"Yeah," I tell her.

"Do you like to dance?"

"Yes," I say. "I love it."

The man comes back to us. Other people start getting into the river, others say they're going to stay here on the shore. Maybe in a little while the river won't be so strong, so angry.

"I'm going to carry her for you," the man says to my cousin.

"And how are you going to do that?" the old woman butts in.

"I'm going to carry her up high," says the man, "with my arms up."

"The river will carry her away," says the woman. "It's too dangerous. And anyway, if you're carrying the girl in your arms, how are you going to hold on to the cabuya?"

"The other guys will help me," the man replies, and turns

around, ignoring her. "If you want, I'll carry her for you," he tells my cousin. "But it has to be now. I'm going to cross over now and there are some other people who can help me."

My cousin looks at me. I nod my head.

"Thank you," says my cousin.

"Thank me when we get to the other side," the man says. "You can't take anything, no backpacks, nothing, leave it all here. And take off your shoes."

I bend down to take off my shoes and then my cousin passes the baby to me so she can take hers off. The baby isn't crying anymore. I think she's tired of crying. Her eyes are open and she's clenching her little fists as if she's got a stomachache. She yawns.

"Nothing's going to happen," I tell my cousin. "You see how lucky you are? What does that man get out of helping you? He could easily leave you here with the baby and just worry about getting to the other side himself."

"It's amazing," my cousin says, "how people help you."

There was a boy we met on the train who helped us out every time the gangs got on. They wanted us to pay them to let us pass, and the boy helped us so that we didn't have to pay. He looked after us. Who knows how he did it or what he said to them. He helped us so much. I even thought that he might have had a crush on my cousin, but she told me she wasn't in the right frame of mind to think about a boyfriend. And then there were all those people standing by the train tracks who threw food to you when you went past. Rice and bean burritos. Sandwiches.

We walk up to the riverbank and a few people start to get in, all in a line, holding on to the cabuya.

"How long will it take?" my cousin asks the man.

"If we're quick, about fifteen minutes," he replies.

"It takes twenty minutes at least," the old woman butts in again.

I put my feet in the water and the cold surges through my whole body: It's true, the water really is freezing. We get in slowly, gripping on to the cabuya, me first, my cousin behind me, and then the man with the baby in his arms, with two other men helping him, sort of holding him up.

"The most important thing is not to get nervous," says the man. "Don't you worry about the little girl, nothing's going to happen to her," he tells my cousin.

We carry on walking, the water up to our knees, our thighs, our bellies. Soon we can't touch the bottom anymore. The river pushes us forward, trying to drag us away, angrily. The cold numbs our legs, our arms; it's hard to keep breathing. Every now and then I swallow some water, but I don't let go of the cabuya.

"Don't let go of the cabuya!" someone shouts. "Hold on tight!"

Some people start to cry. Others shout that they can't do it, that the river is going to carry them away. We're in the middle now, and you can't see the banks any longer. But I look back, and by the light of the moon I see my cousin's baby high up, the man's strong arms protecting her, a little baby girl crossing the border, high above the water.

BEF

AND

ORE

AFTER

MARIANA

THE SOUP

At my grandmother's house there was a mother duck that had just had eighteen ducklings and a chick, because me and my brothers and sisters had done an experiment: We put a chicken's egg in with the rest of her clutch so she would incubate it, and the duck didn't notice. She had a little chick which thought it was a duckling, because it could see that all its brothers and sisters were ducklings. But then one day when we weren't watching, our biggest dog ate the mother duck and left the chick and all the little ducklings orphans.

This was before my brothers went to the United States. First my older brother went, then I was going to go with my younger brother, but in the end only my younger brother could go, and I had to stay and wait some more. But now it's almost my turn. My mom promised us this when she went to the United States.

"Now, don't you think I'm going to forget you," she told us. "If I don't come back, I'll send for you."

Now it's only me left. I'm waiting for the phone call: My grandmother says it'll come soon and that when they call me she's going to cook me a special meal to say goodbye, and she'll invite all my aunts. I lived with my aunts before coming to live in my grandmother's house. At first, I lived for two years with my mom's brother's wife, my mom's sister-in-law. Then I lived for one more year with my mom's youngest sister.

"Mommy, what are you going to cook?" I ask my grandmother, because I call my grandmother Mommy. I call my mommy Mommy, too, obviously.

But she won't tell me.

"It's a surprise," she says.

— — —

Sometimes I try to imagine my mother living in the United States, and now my brothers, too. But I can't, really, because I don't know what things are like over there. I want it to look like those commercials on TV, those before-and-after ads. Like someone who had no hair, and now they do. That kind of thing. I don't know how my life is going to change when I go to the United States, but I'd really like to know what *I'll* be like in a few years' time.

— — —

In my grandmother's house all the animals are loose except for one, a rooster my grandmother keeps in a cage because when it sees a stranger go into the house it runs out and starts trying to peck them. One time it pecked me a couple times, and my grandmother decided to put it in a cage, because it's so fierce. It's practically a dog, minus the barking.

"That rooster's a lot like your dad," says Mommy, my *grandmother*, I mean.

I don't know that much about my dad. All I know is that he left. That he's married to another woman and now he takes care of his stepchildren and a couple of his own kids. He lives in Guatemala, though I don't know where, and I don't know what he does, either. He used to come and see me only when it was my birthday, but my mom had to send him money to make him come and see me, otherwise he wouldn't show.

— — —

When my two brothers were still here, the thing we liked most was to go exploring up on the hill. We'd go out with my two cousins and we'd take salt and lime to eat with the fruits we'd pick up there. Soft green mangoes. And green jocotes, too. We didn't do much else, just went to school or sat around at home. We couldn't buy much because we didn't have any money, only enough to get by.

My mommy here in Guatemala used to work by helping out at a restaurant, and I don't know why but whenever she was paid, there were always some people who'd take the money from her, like they knew the date she was paid, and they'd follow her home. Sometimes she didn't even notice: She'd reach for her bag and realize she was just carrying the handles, that they'd simply sliced the rest of the bag off.

Here in Guatemala you can't really have luxuries because people notice you've got nice things and they demand a payment from you. You can't have earrings or necklaces. Once my mom sent me earrings from the United States and then they disappeared. I never saw them again.

— — —

My mommy lives in New York now, and she's with someone else and she's already had two other kids with him. Before that she lived in Miami and worked in a hotel until she met this man there, who my mom says will be my stepfather when I go and live with them. My stepfather is from Guatemala, too, and he has two kids who live here. He and my mom have been together for a few years now and he's the one who sends the money back, because my mom doesn't always work.

The other day my brothers called me on the phone and I asked them what our stepfather was like. They told me he treated them well, but that he didn't let them watch TV in Spanish. They only watched TV in English so they'd learn the language more quickly. I know I'll learn English quickly. At school I always have the highest grades. The teachers say I've got something in my head that means I can understand numbers quickly. I'd like to be an accountant when I grow up.

My dream has always been to study, to be someone important—not to be famous, but just to be able to get by.

— — —

My grandmother says I'm leaving tomorrow. A woman is going to come for me and first I have to stay with her for a few days until all the people in the group who are going to leave together are there. She called my aunts and my cousins to come and eat with us so that I could say goodbye. She made a delicious soup, with vegetables, chicken, and rice. Later that evening when I was putting things in my backpack for the journey, I realized that the rooster had escaped. I looked for it, but it wasn't in its cage. I looked all over the house, but I couldn't find the rooster anywhere. I went to look for my grandmother.

"Mommy," I said, "I can't find the rooster."

She chuckled before replying.

"Did you look in your belly?" she said.

I remembered the soup and started to cry.

THE LETTER

It was nearly Christmas the day my stepfather came into the house and gave me the letter. He told me it was from a university.

My mom was there, too, and she stood waiting for me to open it. I'm still in high school, but I graduate next year.

"What are you waiting for—open it!" said Mommy.

It was a letter from Harvard inviting me to visit the campus, to see if I'd be interested in studying there. My mom and stepdad were really pleased, although they know I can't go and study there because I don't have any papers. Plus it's really expensive, and I don't have social security to apply for a scholarship. My mom told me she was so proud of all my hard work. I do want to go to a college, just not one that's expensive.

Some people from a local college came to my high school and asked to speak to the twenty students with the highest grades, and from there they picked fifteen of us. They asked me if I wanted to start university early. And so now, as well as high school, I study for a few days a week at this college. I'm studying to be a doctor. I can either carry on studying there or use the credits to study somewhere else. If I do another two years then I'll be a nurse, or I can carry on to be a family doctor, or for a bit longer still if I want to specialize.

The day I received the letter, we were about to put up the Christmas tree. It wasn't a big tree and we didn't have that many decorations, but it looked really pretty. We can't have a tree like the ones on television because we're poor, but we're decent poor people.

When we were decorating the tree I remembered *the home*. I'd been caught when I crossed the border on December 23 and I had to spend my first ever Christmas in the United States in the freezer. Then they sent me to a home where, every now and then, they'd take us outside for a walk. In between Christmas and New Year's, we went to look at other houses in the neighborhood. We went to see how they were decorated. They got a van and put a few of us in it, and they drove us around. We sat in the van and looked at those houses from a distance: the lights, the decorations, the statues of Santa Claus, the reindeer. As I looked at all those lights, sometimes I felt sad thinking I'd never be inside a house like that. But now I am inside one, and I'm happy. And I hope that no one ever makes me leave.

TO
THiS

DAY

ABRIL

WHEN I WOKE UP I WAS COMPLETELY NAKED AND I HAD AN awful headache, and to this day, my head still hurts. They tell me I have a fracture in my head. They did an X-ray and there was a kind of crack in my skull. Every week I have an appointment with the neurologist who gives me medicine to control the pain in my head.

I picked up my clothes from where I'd thrown them on the floor and got dressed. Later, when I got home, I didn't tell my mom anything. I spent nearly a year like that, crying every day, crying because of what had happened to me. My mom could see that I kept fainting all the time, I had bad headaches, and even my hair was falling out because of all the stress. I could barely sleep; I had nightmares all the time. I would dream about those people. This went on until one day I made up my mind and I told my mom what had happened to me, and I told her I didn't want to live there anymore and that the people who had done those bad things to me were threatening me. My mom told my dad, and then he decided that I had to leave Honduras and come here, to New York, where he's been living since 2004. This was in May 2014. I thought that life here would be safer and that nothing bad would happen to me, so I decided to come.

I left on a bus, and then from Mexico I took a train, La Bestia—that's what they call the train—and one day I nearly fell off it. I was about to fall onto the tracks, but nothing happened, thank God. During the journey we went past all these good-hearted people. When the train stopped they'd come over and give us sandwiches, water. Sometimes they gave us chicken and tortillas.

The people I took the trip with were nice. We laughed together; we even laughed about when I nearly fell off the train: I was trying to climb up onto the freight car and I almost fell, and they all laughed, and so did I. And we laughed when my shoes fell apart: I'd walked so much they just broke.

I don't know what I would have done without them. They really helped me; they saved me, though I'm not sure how. Some people tried to kidnap us in Mexico: they told us we had exactly one day to pay the toll, and if we didn't pay, they'd blow off every single finger on our hands. When we took the train in Veracruz, that's when the criminals got on. They had a Taser with them for shocking people. There were three of them, and two policemen with them as well. The policemen saw me fainting because I was scared, and they didn't do anything. The police were working with the criminals. Before I passed out, I saw the thugs giving money to one of the policemen. They said that if we didn't pay a bond we couldn't stay on the train. We said we'd already paid it. But they made us get off and wouldn't let us back on again.

That was in Orizaba. They made us get off the train and said they wouldn't let us on again until they'd made sure that we'd paid. We went to a hotel and they came with us, and two of them stayed behind to make sure no one escaped. Then one of them tried to grab me to get the money we owed them. He said that he liked me and wanted the others to sell me as a trade-off. Another one dragged me over to where he was and hit me round the head with a gun. In the end I don't know what happened or whether my friends had to pay more money, but after this they let us go and we got on a bus and went to Mexico City.

I don't know if I've been unlucky to meet such bad people. There was a really horrible woman working in the freezer, too. When Immigration first stopped me, they sent me to a freezer and then I was transferred to another one in Nogales, Arizona. All they gave me there was a green mattress and a sort of aluminum blanket. Oh God, but there was a woman working there who was so mean—she told me I was a useless beggar. Just because I had grabbed a carton of juice and a peanut cracker, she told me I was a useless beggar. She said that all black people who come here are bums. And I replied: *I'm black and proud.*

Then when they sent me off to my dad's I had to go to court to see if I could stay or if they were going to deport me. My dad never told me about this country, about what the United States was like, how the people live here—he just said that it was all work and study, work and study, work and study. My dad is a bus mechanic and now he's married to another woman and he has other kids. When he came to pick me up from the airport, I didn't believe it was him because he looked so different. I didn't recognize him anymore.

In court they asked me lots of questions. They wanted to know what my life was like back in Honduras. I told them I'm from a little village, two hours from San Pedro Sula, that I lived there with my mom and my two little brothers. In Honduras I finished the twelve school grades, which is like graduating high school, I said. I liked to go to school, I told them; I was a good student.

On the weekends I helped my mom. We sold coconut bread on the beach. We walked along the beach selling it; we took a pana with us, which is like a basket you carry on your head. Back home in the village there's a beach and lots of tourists come from San Pedro Sula and Tegucigalpa.

I also told them that I came over from Honduras in 2014; all I remember is that it was the month of May, I don't recall the exact date it was when I left. I was sixteen.

And in court they wanted to know why I came, what the

reason was for me coming to the United States. I had to tell them that lots of things had happened to me there. That I was sexually abused when I was walking home from school. I used to study for an hour in the village where I lived, and I was attacked when I was coming home from school because I'd stayed later than usual that day.

Everyone had gone home already, and so I had to walk almost half an hour to catch the bus and it was nearly dark, and I was alone, crossing an airfield that doesn't get used anymore. I was just walking across it, and that's where the bad people were waiting for me. There were three of them, and they punched me in the head, and to this day I suffer from headaches. I don't know what happened afterward. I'd never walked that way before; I just did it because it was the fastest route to get the bus home.

"What do you think would happen if you went back to your country?" they asked me in court. "Are you afraid of going back?" I told them that I'm not as afraid as before, because I'd started going to church and that I had spoken to the pastor, and she told me to forget everything that had happened to me. I was beginning to forgive the people who did those things to me. And gradually I did forget. I was seeing a psychologist; I was forgetting about it all bit by bit. But in court, they wanted to know if I might still be in danger in case they were to deport me and I had to go and live in Honduras again. I told them that I was in danger, that the bad people who did those things to me had threatened me, and I said that if I told anyone what they'd done they would kill me, and I was terrified of this.

I hadn't seen these bad people before, but after what happened, they were always hanging around outside my school, and that made me more afraid. Every day, when the bell rang and we all came out, they would drive past in a car. Whenever I got out early I would get straight onto the bus and I could see them driving past. Every time this happened I would hide under the seat on the bus. I recognized the car, the license plate, but I never reported it to the police. I never told the police anything because I was scared that they would kill me and my brothers and sisters, kill my family, because they told me they knew where I lived. That's why I'm so afraid.

I also told them in court that sometimes I talk to my Honduran friends on Facebook. They tell me that last week the gang killed four people in the village where I used to live. Things are the same, my friends say; they go into the houses to steal. The burglars go into the house when you're sleeping, give you a kind of powder that sends you into a deep sleep, and when you wake up, the house is empty as a ballroom.

In court they approved my case and now I've got my papers. Soon I'll be able to apply for citizenship. I feel safer here: When I walk down the street I feel safe, no more worrying about bad people attacking me again. The only sad thing is that I really miss my family. My mom is in the hospital at the moment; she's anemic and she's been hospitalized for over two months. She's got a bad heart and one day it stopped, and they had to revive her in the hospital. When I spoke on the phone with her, all she said was that she was not going to leave this world without seeing me again, that her dying wish was to see me again.

I've been studying English, but it's been quite hard. Mainly because of my headaches. To this day my head still hurts. I was in the hospital here in Lincoln for almost three weeks for a really bad headache. But now my English has gotten better and in September I'm going to go to university. I have to do four years of a bachelor's degree so I can be a lawyer. I'm so happy I'm going to university. It's something I've always wanted, to be someone in life, to be an example for my brothers and sisters.

I had a dream.

I dreamed that I was defending people.

I was a human rights lawyer.

I've dreamed about that quite a few times.

Payment Receipt

Thomas Branch (WPL-THO)
(219) 926-7696
https://wpl.lib.in.us
Sunday, December 15, 2019 2:15:25 PM

Title   : Fifty shades of Grey
Reason   : Overdue Item - CHRG
Charge   : $0.20

Total charges : $0.20
Paid   : $0.20

Account balance: $0.00

Items must be returned to the library
and checked in before closing on the
date(s) due.
Thank you!

ACKNOWLEDGMENTS

I would like to thank the following people and organizations, without whom writing this book would have been impossible: Ana Puente, Tessie Borden, Rebecca Sosa, Valeria Luiselli, Eve Stotland, Amy Joseph, Lorilei Williams, Joanna Furmanska, Andrew Craycroft, CARECEN Los Angeles, and The Door. I would specially like to thank Michael Benoist, who gave me the original idea for this book.

ABOUT THE REFUGEES

Nicole and Kevin ("Where Are Your Kids?" and "I'd Rather Die Trying to Get Out") were born in Guatemala in 2004 and 1998, respectively. They immigrated to the United States in 2014, when they were ten and sixteen. They currently live with their mother, stepfather, and siblings in the San Fernando Valley, California.

Kimberly ("Now I'm Going to Sleep for a Bit") was born in El Salvador in 2000. She immigrated to the United States when she was fourteen, in 2014. She currently lives with her mother, stepfather, and siblings in Hempstead, New York.

Santiago and **Daniel** ("The Other Side Means the Other Side" and "How We Were Going to Get There") were born in El Salvador in 1999 and 2004, respectively. They immigrated to the

United States in 2014, when they were fifteen and ten. They currently live with their mother in Queens, New York.

Dylan ("It Was Like Cotton, but When I Touched It, It Was Just Ice") was born in El Salvador in 2004. He immigrated to the United States in 2014, when he was ten. He currently lives with his mother, stepfather, and brother in Los Angeles, California.

Alejandro ("There Are Snakes Out There") was born in Guatemala in 1996. He immigrated to the United States when he was fifteen, in 2012. He currently lives with his uncle in Queens, New York.

Miguel Ángel ("He and I Got Along Really Well") was born in El Salvador in 1997. He immigrated to the United States in 2014, when he was seventeen years old. He currently lives with his uncle in New York.

Kayla ("La Cabuya") was born in Honduras in 2001. She emigrated with her cousin and her eight-month-old niece in 2014, when she was thirteen years old. She currently lives with her aunt and uncle, her cousins, and her niece in the Bronx, New York.

Mariana ("Before and After") was born in Guatemala in 1997. She immigrated to the United States in 2011, when she was fourteen. She currently lives with her mother, stepfather, and brothers in Queens, New York.

Abril ("To This Day") was born in Honduras in 1997. She immigrated to the United States in 2014, when she was seventeen. She currently lives with a foster family in New York.

GLOSSARY

p. 27. **Salvatrucha**: Also known as MS-13, this is one of several gangs mentioned in the book, and one that exists both in the U.S. (it originated in Los Angeles in the 1980s) and El Salvador, where many of its members are from. Like most gangs, it often uses extortion, which it calls "tax" or "rent," to get money from people, and if they refuse to pay, they or their family members can be killed.

p. 27. **The 18th**: Another particularly violent gang which also started in the States, sometimes known as the 18th Street Gang, Barrio 18, or Mara 18 (*mara* means gang, and mareros are gang members).

p. 31. **Pupusa**: A thick corn tortilla stuffed with a savory filling.

p. 35.   **El Meche:** This character's name means "lock of hair."

p. 43.   **Federales:** This refers to a particular police force in Mexico, typically heavily armed, and is not the same as the U.S. slang term *feds,* although they are sometimes referred to as "the Mexican feds" by the U.S. media and law enforcement agents.

p. 46.   **The Zetas:** A notorious drug cartel from Mexico, one of the largest in the country, which was founded by corrupt members of the military and police.

p. 73.   **Música norteña:** A Mexican genre of music, similar to corridos and polka, named for its northern origins and featuring accordions, the bajo sexto (Mexican "sixth bass"), and a stately dance beat.

p. 110.   **Punta:** A dance and style of music with African beats, originally from the Central American coast of Belize, Honduras, and Guatemala.

p. 119.   **Jocote:** A kind of flowering plant in the same family as the cashew. Its fruit is popular in Central America, and is often eaten when still green, with a sprinkling of salt and lime juice. The flavor of a jocote fruit is said to be similar to a plum—sweet, with a slightly acidic after-taste.

p. 128. **La Bestia** (The Beast): Also known as the *tren de la muerte* (the train of death) and the *tren de los desconocidos* (the train of the unknown ones), this is a network of freight trains crossing Mexico, frequently used by migrants of all ages traveling from Central America to the United States. It makes for a very dangerous journey, and many people die along the way by falling off or getting decapitated.

FURTHER READING

United States Strategy for Central America: The United States government's policy on Central American immigration and border security. https://www.state.gov/u-s-strategy-for-central-america/

The United Nations Refugee Agency: A global organization dedicated to protecting the rights of displaced communities and stateless people. https://www.unhcr.org/en-us/claims-from-central-america.html

United Nations International Children's Emergency Fund (UNICEF): UNICEF works in more than 190 countries and territories to save children's lives and defend their rights. The organization is working to understand the refugee crisis in Central America. https://www.unhcr.org/en-us/claims-from-central-america.html

World Vision: An organization dedicated to providing information and resources to support and provide for Central American migrants. https://www.worldvision.org/refugees-news-stories/central-america-migration-facts

Congressional Research Service: *Recent Migration to the United States from Central America: Frequently Asked Questions*: The Congressional Research Service informs the general public about migrations to the United States from Central America, in particular from El Salvador, Guatemala, and Honduras. https://fas.org/sgp/crs/row/R45489.pdf

Hermanos en el Camino (Brothers on the Road): A migrant shelter located in Oaxaca, Mexico. http://www.hermanosenelcamino.org/english.html

One World Play Project: A nonprofit campaign that raises money to distribute One World Futbols to communities with displaced children, including Hermanos en el Camino. https://www.oneworldplayproject.com/refugee-org-and-news/helping-refugees-in-mexico/

Center for Migration Studies: *Point of No Return: The Fear and Criminalization of Central American Refugees*: A report that details the challenges faced by Central American migrants who have returned home after failing to gain asylum in the United States or Mexico. https://cmsny.org/publications/cms-cristosal-report/

Solito, Solita: Crossing the Borders with Youth Refugees from Central America **by Steven Mayers and Jonathan Freedman:** A collection of oral histories that tells—in their own words—the stories of refugees seeking safety in the United States. https://voiceofwitness.org/solito-solita/

We Built the Wall: How the US Keeps Out Asylum Seekers from Mexico, Central America and Beyond by Eileen Truax and **Diane Stockwell:** In this nonfiction book, a Mexican American lawyer discusses corruption in the asylum procedure and despotism in the Mexican government.